ABC's Of Dog Breeds

A is for
AIREDOODLE

B is for
BOLOGNESE

C is for
CANE CORSO

D is for

DACHSHUND

E is for
EPAGNEUL BRETON

F is for
FOX TERRIER

G is for
GOLDEN RETRIEVER

H is for

HAVANESE

I is for

IRISH WATER SPANIEL

J is for

JACK RUSSELL TERRIER

K is for
KERRY BLUE TERRIER

L is for
LABRADOR RETRIEVER

M is for

MINIATURE SCHNAUZER

N is for

NORWEGIAN BUHUND

O is for

OLD ENGLISH SHEEPDOG

P is for

PUG

Q is for

QUEENSLAND HEELER

R is for

ROTTWEILER

S is for
SIBERIAN HUSKY

T is for

TIBETAN

MASTIFF

U is for

USKAY

(AKA Sloughi)

V is for

VIZSLA

W is for

WELSH TERRIER

X is for
XOLOITZCUINTLI
(pronounced "show-low-eats-QUEENT-lee")

Y is for
YORKSHIRE TERRIER

Z is for

ZWERGPINSCHER

(AKA Miniature Pinscher)

FUN FACTS ABOUT DOGS

1. Dogs' noses can sense heat/thermal radiation, which explains why blind or deaf dogs can still hunt.

2. A dog's nose print is unique, much like a person's fingerprint.

3. . Forty-five percent of U.S. dogs sleep in their owner's bed.

4. The Labrador Retriever has been on the AKC's top 10 most popular breeds list for 30 consecutive years—longer than any other breed.

5. Dogs curl up in a ball when sleeping to protect their organs.

6. All puppies are born deaf.

7. Human blood pressure goes down when petting a dog. And so does the dog's.

8. Dogs are not colorblind. They can see blue and yellow.

9. Dogs have about 1,700 taste buds. We humans have between 2,000–10,000.

10. The Bloodhound's sense of smell is so accurate that the results of its tracking can be used as evidence in a court of law.

https://www.akc.org/expert-advice/lifestyle/dog-facts/